THE CARPENTER BROTHERS • LUCAS ELLIOTT

MOOSE

The herbivore your mother warned you about!

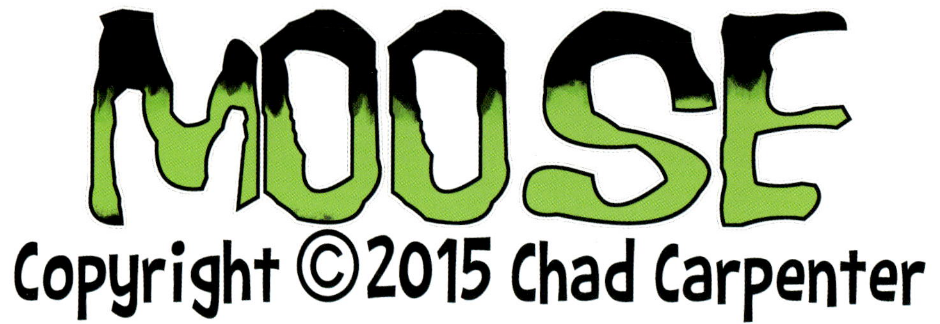

Published by
TUNDRA & ASSOCIATES, INC.
PO Box 871354
Wasilla, Alaska 99687

For additional copies of this or other fine MOOSE or TUNDRA merchandise, please visit:

moosethemovie.com or tundracomics.com

First Printing June 2015
ISBN: 978-1-62343-965-1

THE CARPENTER BROTHERS • LUCAS ELLIOTT

MOOSE

To Matt!

Elliott '18

ONE HUNDRED YEARS AGO...

DEEP WITHIN THE WILDS OF ALASKA, A SHAMAN OF A LOST TRIBE CHANTS THE ENCHANTED WORDS OF THE SPIRIT WORLD...

THUMP!

WHAM!!

CRASH!
CRUNCH!

THE POWER
OF HIS
WORDS GROW
STRONGER...

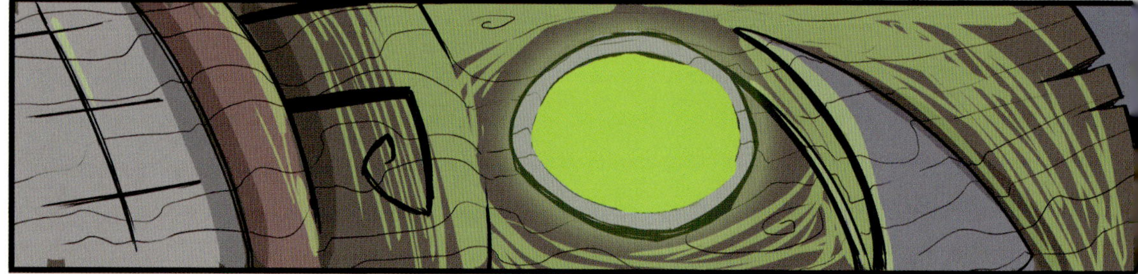

RAWWWR!!!

THE BEAST SINKS SLOWLY INTO THE ABYSS...

AS LONG AS THE TOTEM EXISTED, THE CREATURE WOULD REMAIN BOUND TO THE UNDERWORLD.

GANGRENE GULCH
POP. 243
PRESENT DAY...

POP!
POP!

PSHHH!

HA! THAT WAS BEAUTIFUL!
DANG IT! YOU GOT IT IN MY BEER!

WE BETTER GATHER SOME WOOD, IT'LL BE GETTING DARK SOON.
YEP.. *GULP GULP* RIGHT BEHIND YA!

YOU GONNA HELP OR WHAT?
I'M LOOKING FOR THAT PERFECT PIECE.

WE'RE GOING TO **BURN** IT. JUST GRAB SOMETHING!
DON'T WORRY. I'LL FIND SOMETHING.

I'M HEADING BACK. DON'T TAKE TOO LONG.

THUMP!

WHAT THE...?

'BOUT TIME.
I FOUND IT!

WHAT IS THAT?!

I TOLD YOU I'D FOUND THE PERFECT PIECE OF WOOD.

DUDE, THIS IS A TOTEM. AND AN UGLY ONE AT BEST...

DID YOU SEE THAT?! I THINK THE EYES JUST GLOWED!
WHAT?
WE'RE BOTH AS TOASTED AS THIS DOG. WE'D SEE ABOUT ANYTHING TONIGHT.

FWOOOMP!

'NUFF WEIRDNESS FOR ONE NIGHT. I'M HEADING TO BED.
I THINK I'LL MAKE A PIT STOP FIRST.
WATCH FOR BEARS AND KEEP YOUR DISTANCE.
WHATEVER.
RUSS, GO FIND YOUR OWN TREE.

TRAVIS, I *SAID* KEEP YOUR DISTANCE.
CRACK

MWRRF
ENOUGH WITH THE GRUNTING!

MWRRGH!
GOOD HEAVENS! GET MORE *FIBER* IN YOUR DIET!

AHHHHHHHHHH!!

Welcome to
Gangrene Gulch
Flannel Capit
of the World!

PARK RANGER HQ

PARK RANGER HQ

AAHHHH!!

HELP! CALL 911!!

WHAT'S THE FUSS? WHO'S HURT?

I THINK SHE'S DEAD!

WHO, EDNA? SHE'S DEAD ALRIGHT.

DEAD ASLEEP. SHE'S WHAT YOU CALL A VIOLENT NARCOLEPTIC. SHE'S OUR DISPACHTER & SECRETARY. TYPES LIKE THE WIND.

HOW LONG HAS SHE BEEN ASLEEP?

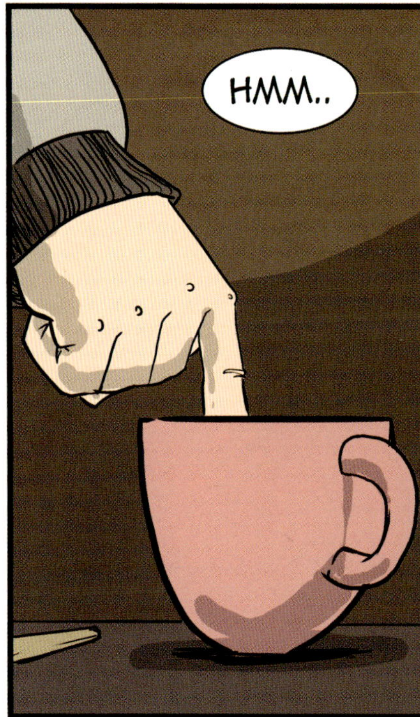
HMM..

I'D SAY ABOUT 45 MINUTES.
SLURP

NEW GUY?
WELCOME TO GANGRENE GULCH. I'M MIKE, THE HEAD RANGER.
ZACK. ZACK DEL POLLO.

SO, WHAT DID YOU MEAN BY VIOLENT NARCOLEPTIC.
LET'S JUST SAY SHE TENDS TO WAKE UP ON THE WRONG SIDE OF THE BED.

LET'S HEAD OUT FOR SOME LUNCH AND LET HER SLEEP IT OFF. I'LL FILL YOU IN ON THE JOB AND THE AREA.
UH, YEAH.. SOUNDS GOOD.

SWEET DREAMS, EDNA.

HOLY!

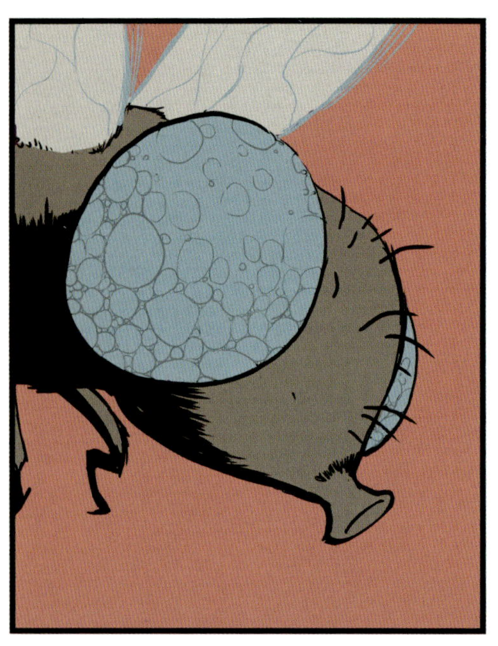

ZATT!!
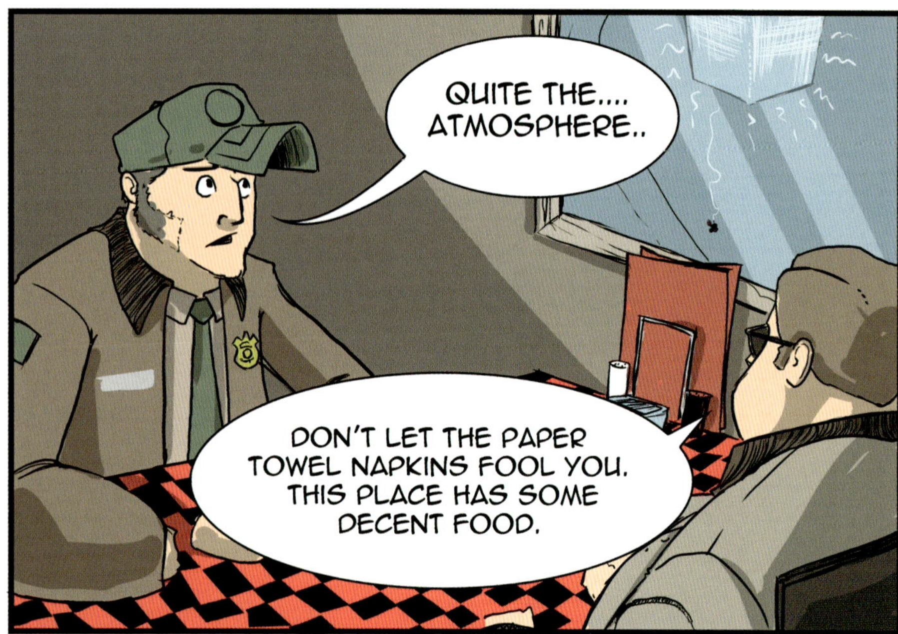
QUITE THE.... ATMOSPHERE..
DON'T LET THE PAPER TOWEL NAPKINS FOOL YOU. THIS PLACE HAS SOME DECENT FOOD.

AND THERE'S BEEN ONLY ***ONE*** CASE OF FOOD POISONING THIS MONTH.

HERE'S THE WAITER NOW.
CAN I TAKE YOUR ORDER, MONSIEURS?

I'LL HAVE THE TOMATO BISQUE WITH THE FRESH SALTINE GARNISH AND MY USUAL COFFEE.

VERY GOOD.... AND YOU MONSIEUR?

THE PUPPET, TALK TO THE PUPPET.

I'LL... I'LL HAVE THE SAME.

WHAT'S THE DEAL WITH THE PUPPET?!

ALFONZ? HE'S NOT YOUR NORMAL GANGRENE GULCH FOLK.
HE'S A BIT MORE REFINED THAN MOST HERE.

YOUR COFFEE AND SOUPS, MONSIEURS.

FRESH GROUND PEPPER?

UM, NO THANKS..

VERY GOOD. JUST CALL FOR ALFONZ IF YOU REQUIRE ANYTHING ELSE.

HE'S GOOD.

LUNCH WILL BE GOOD. GEORGE IS THE COOK TODAY.

SO, THE GUY WITH THE PUPPET IS GEORGE?

NO, THE PUPPET IS GEORGE. I HAVE NO IDEA WHO THE OTHER GUY IS.

ZZATTTZZ!

IT LOOKS GOOD. GUESS I'LL...
SPLOOT!

ON SECOND THOUGHT, I'M NOT TOO HUNGRY...

LOOKS LIKE WE GOT SOME CAMPERS UP HERE
ASK IF THEY'VE SEEN ANY MOOSE!
I'VE GOT A BAD FEELING ABOUT THIS...
ME TOO..

SOMEONE SHOULD CHECK THINGS OUT.
YES, YOU SHOULD.

THUMP!

AAAAIIIEEE!!!
BLAM!!

YOU THINK HE'S DEAD? HE LOOKS BEAT TO DEATH.
IF HE WASN'T, YOUR BULLET DID THE JOB.

UGH, I THINK I'M GONNA BE SICK.

I'LL BE RIGHT BACK!
DON'T WANDER OFF TOO FAR

YEP. DEFINITELY GONNA LOSE IT...

WHAT THE...?!

HERE'S ANOTHER ONE!!

WE NEED TO GET TO TOWN AND LET SOMEONE KNOW WHAT WE'VE FOUND

WHY DON'T I GO SHOW YOU THE SIGHTS? THAT SHOULD KILL 5 MINUTES OR SO.

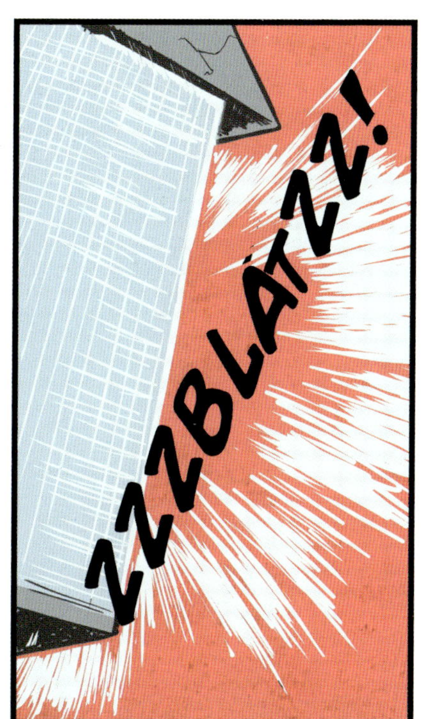
ZZZBLATZZ!

SPLUT

YEAH... THAT SOUNDS LIKE A GOOD IDEA.

HMM, MUST BE THE START OF BAT SEASON.

DID YOU BOYS ENJOY YOUR LUNCHES?

IT WAS GREAT, LIZ.
OH YEAH, THE COFFEE WAS PASSABLE AND THE FRIED BAT SOUP WAS A NICE SURPRISE.

OH DEAR, THEODORE WILL BE SO SAD TO HEAR WE LOST ANOTHER MILKER.

WAIT! WHAT?! HOW DO YOU MEAN A "MILKER"?

THEODORE MILKS THE BATS FOR OUR COFFEE CREAM. HE COMES FROM A LONG LINE OF BAT MILKERS. HE'LL BE SO UPSET.

DID I HEAR MY NAME?

SHHHH.

THIS IS THE WEIRDEST DAY EVER...
I GUESS I'LL GIVE YOU THE TOUR. SUPERMARKET OVER THERE..
LIBRARY JUST UP THERE...
AND THAT BESIDE IT IS CITY HALL, JAIL AND DMV...
THAT'S IT UNLESS YOU WANT TO SEE THE SEWAGE LAGOON.
Grease Trap Cafe
If it ain't fried, it ain't food.

THAT'LL REQUIRE A TRIP TO THE FAIRGROUNDS.

AFTERNOON, NORM. MEET ***ZACK***, OUR NEW PARK RANGER.

IS HE AN ALIEN?
HMM, I DONT BELIEVE SO, ***ARE*** YOU?

UH, NO?!

HMPPHHFF! JUST WHAT YOU'D EXPECT AN ALIEN TO SAY.

YOU WATCH HIM. IF HIS TENTACLES TRY TO SNEAK INTO ONE OF YOUR ORIFICES, DON'T SAY I DIDN'T TRY TO WARN YOU.
THANKS FOR THE TIP, NORM.

IS IT ME OR IS THIS WHOLE PLACE NUTS?
WELL, WE DO HAVE OUR SHARE OF CHARACTERS I ADMIT, BUT MOST OF THEM ARE DECENT FOLK.

WAIT A MINUTE! OUR DISPATCHER IS A VIOLENT NARCOLEPTIC, WE ATE AT A BAT-ZAPPING RESTAURANT RUN BY ONE GUY AND HIS MERRY BAND OF PUPPETS AND THAT CRAZY GUY THINKS I'M AN ALIEN WITH TENTACLE-POKING POWERS!
LIKE I SAID, WE HAVE A FEW ODD DUCKS. GANGRENE GULCH IS THE MIDDLE OF NOWHERE. YOU HAVE TO BE A LITTLE DIFFERENT, BUT NO ONE IS CRAZY.

WHOOP! WHOOP! WHOOP!

NOW, RODNEY ON THE OTHER HAND... WE'VE CONSIDERED HAVING HIM TESTED..

A DOUBLE FATALITY INVOLVING
TWO MALE CAMPERS WHO
WERE MESSING AROUND
ON FOUR-WHEELERS.

REALLY? YOU HAVE A
CODE FOR ***THAT***?

ALASKA
MOOSE1

SHOULDN'T WE CALL THE TROOPERS?
NO TROOPERS AROUND FOR A HUNDRED MILES. WE ARE THE CAVALRY.

LOOKS LIKE WE'RE HERE.

WHO'S THAT?!
OH, THAT'S SAM. THE CORONER'S ASSISTANT.

CHUBBA-WANNA -DOODY.

HOWDY, SAM!

HI! YOU GUYS FIGURED OUT WHAT HAPPENED YET?
JUST GOT HERE. SAM, THIS IS ZACK, THE NEW RANGER.

HI ZACK, NAME'S SAMANTHA GREEN. I'M THE ASSISTANT CORONER, CSI, AND LIBRARIAN FOR GANGRENE GULCH AS WELL AS THE KNITTING CLUB PRESIDENT.

YOU WEAR PRETTY HATS.. I MEAN MANY HATS.

UH.. YEAH.. SHOULDN'T WE GO LOOK AROUND?
RIGHT BEHIND YOU!

THE CALLER SAID THERE WAS ONE BODY IN THE TENT AND ANOTHER ABOUT A HUNDRED YARDS OVER BY THE TREE LINE.

WOW! LOOKS LIKE A MOOSE DID THIS.

YOU CAN SEE THE OBVIOUS HOOF PRINTS ON HIS HEAD, AAAANNNDDD....APPARENTLY THIS MOOSE WAS ARMED. THERE'S A BULLET WOUND.
UH, YEAH. ONE OF THE CALLERS SAID THEIR RIFLE ACCIDENTALLY WENT OFF WHEN THEY SAW THE BODY.

FROM WHAT THEY SAID, THE OTHER BODY IS OVER THAT WAY.

CAREFUL, WE DON'T KNOW WHAT WE'RE DEALING WITH. THE PERP COULD STILL BE AROUND.

LIKE A FLESH EATING MOOSE?
A WHAT?
SOUNDS DRAMATIC. YOU KNOW, LIKE SOME CHEESY HORROR FILM. BUT REALLY, A BLOOD THIRSTY MOOSE? RIGHT?

UH...YEAH...

WELL, HERE'S **NUMBER 2**.
HE DOESN'T LOOK TOO GOOD.
HAVING A **1200 LB** ANIMAL STOMP ON YOUR HEAD IS A BIT ROUGH ON THE COMPLEXION.

SO ANY IDEA WHY THIS THING WENT ALL TONYA HARDING ON THESE GUYS?
COULDA SPOOKED IT?

IS IT UNUSUAL FOR A MOOSE TO ATTACK AND KILL TWO PEOPLE?
FIRST I'VE SEEN.
ME TOO.

WE'LL HAVE TO EXAMINE CLOSER, BUT I DON'T SEE ANY OTHER OBVIOUS HITS.
NOT THAT IT WAS NECESSARY. THE **HEAD SHOT** DID THE TRICK. LOOKS LIKE THAT THEORY OF A RAMPAGING MOOSE HOLDS UP.

AND IT LOOKS LIKE YOUR **CLEANUP CREW** IS HERE.

SCREEEEECH!
JED & RUPERT'S
YOU MAKE A MESS, WE MAKE IT GO AWAY, INC.
- NO QUESTIONS ASKED -
CLEANUP CREW?
WHEN THERE'S ROAD KILL, THE CLEANUP CREW CLEARS THE CARCASS OFF THE ROAD THEY ALSO DOUBLE AS THE CORONER TRANSPORT TEAM.

GOT A CALL YOU HAD SOME WORK FOR US?
YEAH, TWO BODIES TO THE CORONER'S OFFICE.

UHH, DRESS 'EM OUT FIRST?

NO! DO NOT, I REPEAT, DO NOT DRESS THEM OUT. ONE PIECE.

I MADE THE MISTAKE NOT CLARIFYING WHEN OLD MAN WINSLOW DIED FROM WHAT WE THINK WAS NATURAL CAUSES.

I SAY THINK BECAUSE IT'S KINDA HARD TO AUTOPSY A STEAK FILLET.

TO BE FAIR, THEY'RE DECENT ROAD KILL REMOVAL. NOT MUCH PRACTICE WITH HUMANS AROUND HERE.

SO... THEY **REALLY** CUT UP THE OL' GUY?

PROCESSED AND PACKAGED, TOO. YOU CAN IMAGINE A FUNERAL WITH THE FAMILY SEEING 30 PACKAGES OF MEAT CUTS NEATLY STACKED IN A ***CASKET***.
UH, YEAH. I SUPPOSE **THAT** WOULD BE AN ISSUE.

ESPECIALLY WHEN THERE WERE **50** PACKAGES TO START WITH.

UM, WHERE'D THE OTHER **20** GO?

LET'S JUST SAY WE ***DON'T*** HAVE COMMUNITY BARBECUES ANYMORE.

HEAR FROM YOU LATER, SAM?
TO SERVE AND PROTECT
Gangrene Gulch
Alaska
Park Ranger

AS SOON AS THE AUTOPSY IS DONE.
NICE MEETING YOU, SAM.

I'LL CALL YOU LATER.
REALLY?!

AS SOON AS I GET THE AUTOPSY RESULTS.
OH. GREAT. THANKS...

SEE YOU LATER!

1...2...3...

WHAM!

AGAIN.

MIND IF I HEAD OUT? SUPPOSED TO MEET MY NEW LANDLORD.
NAH. JUST GONNA DO PAPERWORK.
WHERE'D YOU FIND A PLACE? HOUSING IS KINDA SCARCE.

JUST A COUPLE MILES UP THE ROAD. SOUNDS DECENT. OWNER'S NAME IS ***FRANK***.

ANGER HQ
FRANK, EH? GOOD LUCK WITH ***THAT***. TELL FRANK I SAID HI.

WILL DO!

KNOCK
KNOCK

CREAK

YEAH? CAN I HELP YA?

UH... ARE YOU FRANK?

THAT'S WHAT ALL THE RESTRAINING ORDERS SAY.

I CALLED ABOUT THE CABIN WITH THE DELUXE ACCOMMODATIONS.

P-TOOIE!

I'LL GET THE KEYS. THE PLACE IS JUST BACK UP THE ROAD A PIECE. YOU PASSED IT COMING IN.

SLAM!

WEIRD. I DON'T REMEMBER SEEING A CABIN ON THE WAY.

CLICK
GOT THE KEYS. I'LL GO SHOW YOU 'ROUND.

I MUST'VE BEEN ZONING. I DON'T REMEMBER SEEING THE CABIN.

TA-DAH!!

WHERE IS IT? BEHIND THE *SHED*?

THAT'S *NO* SHED, EINSTEIN! THAT'S THE CABIN.

AIN'T IT A LITTLE SMALL?

I PREFER **"QUAINT"**.

OK, EXTREMELY **"QUAINT"**.

HERE WE HAVE THE BEDROOM,

KITCHEN,

LIVING ROOM,

DEN, AND PRIVATE LIBRARY.

WATER IS A 5-GALLON BUCKET YOU TAKE TO TOWN AND FILL UP WHEN YOU **RUN** OUT.

NOW THE "FACILITIES" ARE A PLEASANT 50-FOOT WALK OVER BY THEM TREES.

WE DUG OUT A FRESH 15-FOOT HOLE AND MOVED IT TO A NEW SPOT. GONNA TAKE A LOT OF BURRITOS TO FILL THAT PUPPY UP. FOR QUICK TRIPS, WE INSTALLED A NEW URINAL.

YOU KNOW. THIS IS AN ***AWESOME*** PLACE, BUT I THINK IT'S A LITTLE ***TOO*** AWESOME FOR ME. I'LL GET BACK TO YOU ON IT.

THIS IS THE FIRST RENTAL IN 6 MONTHS, SO UNLESS YOU WANT TO WINTER IN A TENT, I'D ADVISE YOU TO SIGN THE LEASE.

YOU GOT A PEN?

STANLEY! YOU WALKED THE DOG YET?!

HUH?

IF THAT DOG POOPS IN MY SLIPPERS AGAIN, YOU'LL FIND IT UNDER YOUR PILLOW!

ALRIGHT, MAW!

YOU GOING?!
I'M GOING, MAW!

C'MON...
DO YOUR BIZ.

AND DONT TAKE TOO LONG EITHER.. OR ELSE.

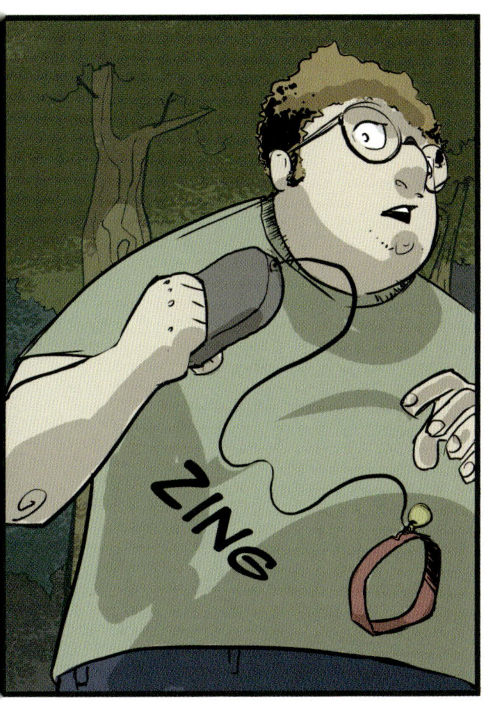
ZING

DOGGIE?

FUNNY, DOG. I'M COMING IN AND YOU'RE GONNA BE REAL SORRY!

YOU'RE GONNA BE REAL SORRY.

LAST WARNING, DOG.
MAC

AAAAAHHHHH!!!

PARK RANGER HQ
NEXT DAY...

OH HI!
YOU MUST BE ZACK.
NICE TO MEET YOU.

UH, YES.. NICE TO MEET YOU TOO. BROUGHT A FEW THINGS FOR MY OFFICE, CAN YOU TELL ME WHERE THAT IS?

OF COURSE, DEAR. JUST RIGHT OVER THERE.

HELP STOP THE SPREAD OF S.T.D.s*
*Salmon Transmitted Diseases
PRACTICE SAFE FISHING

GREAT. RIGHT NEXT TO YOU. SO CLOSE. COOL.

OH YES! WE CAN CHAT UP A STORM. IT'LL BE SO FUN!

OOOOKAY. JUST GONNA ARRANGE A FEW THINGS. (CAUSE I LOVE DODGING COFFEE CUPS...)

I'M KNITTING A PAIR OF SOCKS FOR MY DARLING KITTEN. SHE HAS CIRCULATION PROBLEMS AND HER PAWS GET CHILLY IN THE WINTER. I THOUGHT THEY'D MAKE A NICE CHRISTMAS PRESENT THIS YEAR.

NICE.

THWAK!!

ZZZZZZZZZZ....

ZACK! JUST GOT A MISSING PERSONS CALL!

WHAT'S THAT...?

STIMPLE

KNOCK
KNOCK

WHAT?

MRS. STIMPLE, YOU REPORTED YOUR **SON** MISSING? CAN YOU GIVE US SOME DETAILS?

NOT MUCH TO SAY. HE TOOK THE DOG FOR A WALK AND THAT'S THE LAST I SAW HIM. PROBABLY OFF SMOKING GOOFY PILLS OR WHATEVER KIDS DO THESE DAYS.

IF YOU THINK HE'S OFF SMOKING "GOOFY PILLS", WHY'D YOU CALL **US**?

IT'S HIS TURN TO CLEAN THE TOILET. FIGURED HE'S JUS' TRYIN TO GET OUT OF IT.... AGAIN

WOULD YOU HAPPEN TO HAVE A PHOTO OF HIM, MA'AM?

YEAH, HANG ON A SEC'.

HERE. BUT IT'LL BE HARD TO RECOGNIZE HIM WITHOUT THAT *COUCH* STUCK TO HIS BACKSIDE.

KEEP IT, IF IT'LL HELP.

UH, THANKS. MIND IF WE LOOK AROUND A BIT?

SURE. HE USUALLY TAKES THE DOG AROUND BACK.

SLAM!

GET A FEELING WE'RE WASTING OUR TIME?
AFTER YOU.
YUP. GOT ANYTHING BETTER TO DO?

GET MOVED IN?
YEAH, LIKE I'M LIVING IN AN ELEVATOR WITH A WINDOW. I SWEAR FRANK...
WHINE WHINE

SOUNDS LIKE A DOG.

IT'S COMING FROM THIS WAY!

UUUUHHHHH, DO YOU THINK THIS IS STANLEY?
THAT'D BE MY GUESS.

IN THE PHOTO, HE HAS MORE OF A... HEAD.

NOW WHERE DID THAT HEAD ROLL OFF TO...?

AHH, WHAT HAVE WE HERE?

DOES THIS LOOK LIKE OUR GUY?

UNGHH..

WEIRD.

FROM THE BRUISING, I'D SAY THIS IS ANOTHER MOOSE ATTACK, ALBEIT A ***VICIOUS*** ONE.

YUP, MUST HAVE BEEN ONE TICKED-OFF MAMMA MOOSE? ***FLAT STANLEY*** HERE PROBABLY SPOOKED HER AND HER CALF.

I'LL HAVE THE LOCAL RADIO STATION WARN PEOPLE TO GIVE MOOSE A WIDE BERTH, IF THEY SEE ANY.

I HEAR YOU GOT MORE ***WORK*** FOR US!

YEP. REMEMBER, ***NO*** FIELD DRESSING. THIS ONE COMES IN ***TWO*** PIECES.

HOW LONG DO YOU THINK HE'LL STAY IN SHOCK?
NOT LONG. I'M ABOUT TO BRING HIM AROUND.

ZAP!! CRACK!!

WHAT WAS *THAT?!*
SHOCK THERAPY. PEOPLE PAY GOOD MONEY FOR THAT.

I'LL TRY A FEW MORE TIMES IF HE DOESN'T WAKE UP.

WANT US TO GET THIS'N TOO?
NO! THIS ONE'S OFF LIMITS!!

BETTER GO CHARGE THIS UP.

LATER THAT EVENING, AT THE RANGER STATION...

CLICK

CRUNCH

CRUNCH
CRUNCH
HONK!
HONK!!
SCREECH!
GONNA HAVE TO STRETCH A LITTLE BIT FURTHER...
WHAT THE?!

SCREEEECH!!

CRASH!

CRUNCH!!

OOF! GUESS I BETTER LOOK AROUND.

WHERE'D I PUT THAT FLASHLIGHT..?

CLICK
CLICK

ACK!

WHY I OUGHTA...

LET'S CHECK THE DAMAGE..

CRAP! GOTTA CALL A TOW.

THEY'RE GONNA LOVE THIS STORY,

CRASH!!

AHHH!
SMASH!

WHUMP!

THUMP!
THUMP!
WHUMP!

MWWRRROOOOAARR!

THE NEXT MORNING...

CREAK..

YOU DEAD?

SQUEAL!!

IT'S OK! IT'S OK. AFTER BEING TAZED MULTIPLE TIMES, I WASN'T SURE IF YOU'D STILL BE BREATHING.

SORRY, STILL OUT OF IT A BIT.

EXACTLY, WHY ARE YOU HERE?

CORONER EXAMINED STANLEY'S REMAINS LAST NIGHT. FIGURED WE'D GO GET THE *RESULTS* TODAY.

?
ALRIGHT. JUST LET ME CATCH A QUICK HOT BATH.

*OO*OKAY..

CAN A GUY HAVE A LITTLE *PRIVACY*?

WHATEVER, GUY. I'LL MEET YOU IN THE CAR.

MIKE COMING? PROBABLY WORN OUT FROM SHOCKING ME.
I CALLED BUT HE DIDN'T ANSWER HIS PHONE.

I SHOULD WARN YOU...OUR CORONER IS GOOD...BUT, A BIT ODD.

HEH. WHO IN THIS TOWN *ISN'T*?

Grease Trap Cafe
Employee o' the month
Walk-In Freezer
-keep door locked-
(squirrels like to steal ice cream)
ZACK? ARE YOU *OKAY*?

ZACK, CAN YOU *HEAR* ME?

THIS IS *GEORGE*, OUR CORONER.

MEAT CUTS

IS HE..
IS HE MUTE?

NO... HE'S HAD
A ROUGH WEEK.

ZACK, SAY
SOMETHING!

YOU'RE..
YOU'RE.. THE
CHEF PUPPET.

THAT'S MY
DAY JOB.

BUT THIS.... THIS IS
MY PASSION!
MEAT CUTS

SAM, WE'RE IN A WALK-IN FREEZER OF A RESTAURANT WITH A DEAD BODY.
MEAT CUTS

WELL, YES. IT'S A SMALL TOWN SO GOTTA USE WHAT WE HAVE. AND THERE'S ACTUALLY THREE BODIES.

THE OTHER TWO ARE STACKED OVER WITH THE BURGER PATTIES.

AREN'T YOU WORRIED ABOUT STORING BODIES WITH FOOD?!

THEY'RE DEAD. IT'S NOT LIKE THEY EAT MUCH.

OK, ASIDE FROM THAT. I'M HAVING AN ISSUE WITH THE WHOLE "CORONER" THING.

WHAT EXPERIENCE DOES HE HAVE TO BE AN EXPERT? HOW DO YOU EXPECT ME OR ANYONE ELSE TO TAKE THIS SERIOUSLY?

WELL,I STARTED BY DISSECTING SOCK PUPPETS, THEN MARIONETTES, WORKED MY WAY UP TO THE NEIGHBOR'S CAT. SOON AFTER, I WAS ACCEPTED TO MEDICAL SCHOOL.

YOU WENT TO MEDICAL SCHOOL?

A LOT OF FOLKS DIDN'T THINK IT WAS POSSIBLE BACK THEN. THANKS TO EQUAL RIGHTS, I GOT IN.

BECAUSE... YOU'RE A PU...

YES... I'M IRISH.

ANYWAY, BACK TO THE AUTOPSY. I FOUND HAIRS ON THE VICTIMS, NOT BELONGING TO ANY OF THEM.

SHALL WE TAKE A LOOK?

WOAH, IS THAT...?

OOPS! THIS TASTY LITTLE GUY ALMOST GOT AWAY.

BRATWURST
THERE YOU GO..

I WAS ABLE TO MATCH THE DNA FROM THOSE HAIRS....
TO THE *MURDERER*.

MURDERER? WHO MURDERED THEM?

A MOOSE!!

A MOOSE?! I COULD HAVE TOLD YOU THAT WHEN WE FOUND THEM.

BUT, IT WAS NO ORDINARY MOOSE. IT WAS AN *EVIL* MOOSE.

NO, REALLY.
LET ME EXPLAIN.

MEAT CUTS
HNN

SO JUST HOW EVIL IS THIS MOOSE?

IF EVIL WAS MIDI-CHLORIANS, THIS MOOSE WOULD EQUAL ***THREE*** DARTH VADERS.

THANK YOU FOR WHAT WAS AN EYE-OPENING AND RATHER DISGUSTING EXPERIENCE.

DON'T FORGET TO TRY TODAY'S SPECIAL! SAUERKRAUT & BRATS!
BRATWURST

DID YOU NOTICE ANYTHING ODD IN THERE..?
I'M A LITTLE SURPRISED GEORGE IS *IRISH*.

SAM! HE'S A PUPPET!

YOU KNOW MOST OF THE PEOPLE AROUND HERE, RIGHT?

YEAH, MOST.

ANYONE KNOW ABOUT INDIGENOUS WILDLIFE?
YEAH, A BIOLOGIST.

LET'S GO PAY HIM A VISIT.

Rabid
quirrel
mpground
ty of Gangrene Gulch

ELSEWHERE

IT GOES KINDA LIKE THAT. STILL WORKING ON THE ENDING.

IT WAS DEEP... SPIRITUAL LIKE...

I THINK MY AURA SHIFTED DUDE...

ELSEWHERE, ELSEWHERE...
KNOCK
KNOCK
KNOCK

HELLO? CAN I HELP YOU?

MY NAME IS SAM AND THIS IS ZACK FROM THE RANGER'S OFFICE. ARE YOU NED BUCKHOLTZ THE BIOLOGIST?

WHY, YES. YES, I AM.

NED, WE'VE HAD THREE PEOPLE KILLED RECENTLY AND WE UNDERSTAND YOU SPECIALIZE IN MOOSE RESEARCH.
MIND IF WE ASK YOU SOME QUESTIONS?

SURE. COME ON IN.

WOW, NED. LOOKS LIKE YOUR PLACE COULD DO WITH A WOMAN'S TOUCH
SEEM'S SO.. LABBIE.

OH, I DONT HAVE A GIRLFRIEND CURRENTLY... RECENTLY... ...EVER.

NED, YOU'VE HEARD ABOUT THE RECENT MOOSE TRAMPLING DEATHS?

YEAH, BUT IF THEY'RE SIMPLE MOOSE TRAMPLINGS, WHY COME TO ME?

WELL, THEY MAY NOT BE SO SIMPLE.
MAY I SHOW YOU SOME SCENE PHOTOS?

YOU SAY A MOOSE DID THIS? I'VE SEEN A FEW TRAMPLINGS BUT NEVER...NEVER ANYTHING THIS BRUTAL...

ODD..

WHAT'S ODD?
IT JUST LOOKS A BIT LIKE OVERKILL TO ME.
COULD IT HAVE BEEN A MOTHER MOOSE PROTECTING HER YOUNG?
HMM.. MAYBE.

NED, WHAT EXACTLY IS YOUR EXPERTISE?

MOOSE FLATULENCE AND HOW IT AFFECTS THE AURORA.

WHAT?!

MOOSE FLATULENCE AND HOW IT AFFECTS THE NORTHERN LIGHTS.

THAT'S WHAT I THOUGHT YOU SAID...

I KNOW IT SOUNDS DUBIOUS, BUT LISTEN...

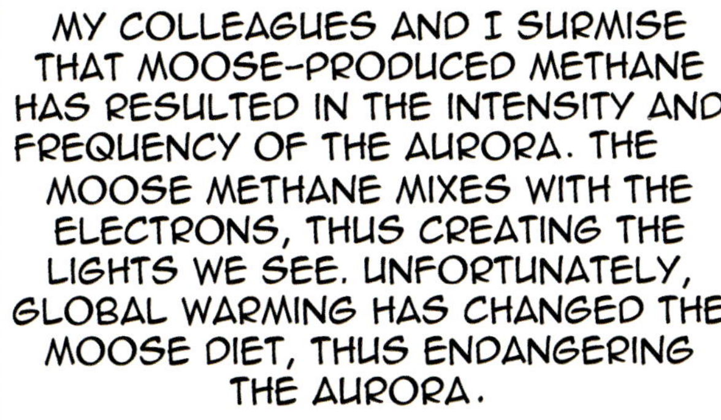
MY COLLEAGUES AND I SURMISE THAT MOOSE-PRODUCED METHANE HAS RESULTED IN THE INTENSITY AND FREQUENCY OF THE AURORA. THE MOOSE METHANE MIXES WITH THE ELECTRONS, THUS CREATING THE LIGHTS WE SEE. UNFORTUNATELY, GLOBAL WARMING HAS CHANGED THE MOOSE DIET, THUS ENDANGERING THE AURORA.

YOU'RE TELLING ME **MOOSE FARTS** CAUSE THE NORTHERN LIGHTS?

IN LAYMAN'S TERMS, YES.

WAIT, THERE ARE LIGHTS OVER THE SOUTH POLE AND NO MOOSE THERE.

PENGUIN FARTS.

SO, WHAT'S WITH ALL THE EMPTY JARS?

THEY'RE NOT EMPTY. THEY'RE SAMPLES. EACH CONTAINS FLATULENCE FROM DIFFERENT SUBJECTS OVER THE YEARS.
WANT TO TRY A SAMPLE?

UH, PASS. ALLERGIES.

SO, HOW DID YOU OBTAIN THESE SAMPLES?

WITH GREAT SACRIFICE. WE LOST A FEW BRAVE SOULS OVER THE YEARS.

THANKS, NED. THIS HAS BEEN VERY... EDUCATIONAL.

YOU KNOW. MOOSE ONLY ATTACK OUT OF DEFENSE. THOSE PHOTOS LOOKED MORE LIKE AN EXTREMELY AGGRESSIVE ATTACK.

WAIT!

COULD I *INTEREST* YOU IN A SHIRT TO SUPPORT THE CAUSE? COFFEE MUGS? BUMPER STICKERS? ***PENNANTS?***
WWW.SAVETHEAURORA.COM
savetheAurora.com
WWW.SAVETHEAURORA.COM

...HUG A TREE, HUG A TREE, DON'T MAKE BATS OUTTA THEM.. HUG A TREE, HUG A TREE, WHAT DID THEY EVER DO TO YOU..?

WOAH...I'M REALLY BEGINNING TO TRIP, MAN...

DUDE. DO YOU KNOW YOU'RE ALL, LIKE... ANTLER-IE?

GASP!
WHAT?
SHH, SHH..
OH MY...
HUH?

HEY, CHILL. I CAN REWORK THE CHORUS...

AHHHH!!!

TWANG!
Rabid Squirrel Campground property of Gangrene Gulch
AHH! OH GOD! HELP!!
NOOO!
RUN!

WHAM

DUDE...

I'M SENSING A LOT OF TENSION IN THE AIR..

NOOOOO!!

WHERE'D EVERYBODY GO?

............?

ACK!!

HEY MAN! PARTY FOUL!!

YOU KNOW DUDE, I'M SENSING SOME SERIOUS AGGRESSION HERE.

PEACE, MAN..

WOAH, BRENT! WHERE'D YOUR HEAD GO?

WOULDN'T YOU BE COOL WITH ONE OF THESE? A CANDY-POOPING MOOSE?

I THINK I'M SET FOR A WHILE. WE GOTTA GO.

DON'T FORGET, THAT'S SAVETHEAURORA.COM!

SO, WHAT DID YA THINK?
BESIDES THE FART-BASED AURORA? DON'T KNOW. BUT THE ATTACKS NOT BEING NORMAL GIVES US SOMETHING TO THINK ABOUT.

I REALLY WISH WE COULD GET AHOLD OF MIKE ON THIS.

BASE TO ZACK. COME IN.

THIS IS ZACK. HEARD FROM MIKE?
NO, BUT WE GOT ANOTHER CALL.

CALLER SAID SOMETHING ATTACKED HIS FRIENDS. HE'S OUT AT RABID SQUIRREL CAMPGROUND. HE SOUNDED STONED OR IN SHOCK. NOT TOO COHERENT.

ROGER THAT. SEE IF YOU CAN FIND MIKE. BETTER CALL THE CLEANUP CREW, TOO.

LOOKS LIKE ANOTHER ATTACK.

WOAH, ARE YOU THE ONE THAT CALLED?
YEAH, ONE OF MY FRIENDS HAD A PHONE.
I DON'T HAVE ONE. THEY KILL BRAIN CELLS.

YEAH, SURE..WELL.. WE WERE JUST SITTING AROUND THE FIRE, SINGING AND ENJOYING NATURE'S BOUNTY.
THEN NATURE CAME OUT AND KICKED OUR BUTTS.

NATURE DID?

YEAH. ONE MINUTE IT'S ALL FINE THEN NEXT THERE'S TIE-DYE & BIRKENSTOCKS FLYING EVERYWHERE!

CAN YOU DESCRIBE WHAT "NATURE" LOOKED LIKE?

YEAH....

AND...

YOU GOTTA UNDERSTAND, I MIGHT NOT HAVE BEEN COMPLETELY LUCID AT THE TIME.. AND I HAD SMOKE IN MY EYES.
CAMPFIRE SMOKE?
UH, YEAH, SURE.

WELL, DO YOUR BEST PLEASE.

UMM... IT WAS *REALLY* TALL.

HAIRY, BUT NOT *HIPPIE* HAIRY.

HUGE ANTLER HORNY THINGS ON ITS HEAD.

SOUNDS LIKE A MOOSE TO ME.

YEAH! A MOOSE. DRESSED LIKE A HOBO?

SO, WE HAVE A TALL, HAIRY, ANTLERED CREATURE THAT RESEMBLES A MOOSE AND DRESSES LIKE A HOBO. ANYTHING *ELSE*?

YES! HE WALKED ON *TWO* LEGS!

KINDA LIKE A MAN-MOOSE THING...
A MOOSETAUR!!

YOU'LL HAVE TO EXCUSE ME. I NEED TO SPEAK TO THE CLEANUP CREW.

SURE.

HI BOYS.
WOO-WE! LOOKS LIKE WE GOT A MESS O' PEOPLE. YOU KNOW WE DON'T DO BULK DISCOUNT, RIGHT?

FINE. WHATEVER. JUST GIVE ME A FEW MOMENTS TO TAKE SOME PHOTOS BEFORE YOU CLEAN IT UP.
DON'T THINK WE GOT ENOUGH BODY BAGS. CAN WE USE TRASH BAGS?

AND ZIPLOCKS. WE JUST FINISHED LUNCH.

NO! I HAVE SOME TARPS IN THE CAR. JUST WAIT.

A FEW MINUTES LATER...
I GOT ALL THE PHOTOS I NEED AND I *THINK* WE FOUND ALL THE PARTS.

HOW MANY OF YOU WERE THERE?
UM...

WELL, IT WAS SIX... AND ME ...EIGHT!
SEVEN!

YEP. THAT MAKES ALL OF THEM.

I'M GONNA TRY MIKE AGAIN.

I THINK I'LL CHECK ON OUR CREW. LET ME KNOW WHAT YOU FIND OUT.

DID YOU GET ALL THE PARTS?

YES, MA'AM. THERE MIGHT BE AN ODD TOE OR FINGER, BUT NOTHING IMPORTANT.

I STILL CAN'T RAISE HIM.
I HOPE HE'S OK.

EAGLE'S NEST
TO BABY EAGLET.

THE CALL SIGN
WASN'T MY IDEA.

GO AHEAD.
WHATCHA GOT,
EDNA.

JUST GOT A CALL THAT
A WRECKED RANGER
VEHICLE WAS SEEN IN A
DITCH AT MILE 5 OF
FROSTBITE ROAD.

THAT'S THE
DIRECTION OF
MIKE'S HOUSE.

FROSTBITE ROAD
MILE 5

SINCE YOU'RE HERE, MAKE YOURSELVES USEFUL.

MIKE?!MIKE?! CAN YOU HEAR ME?

UNH...

ZACK! I THINK HE'S STILL IN THERE.

MIKE! CAN YOU HEAR ME?!
GROAAAN

EDNA! THIS IS ZACK. SEND AN AMBULANCE AND RESCUE TEAM! WE FOUND MIKE PINNED IN HIS TRUCK.

10-4, BABY EAGLET!

RING RING

OK, GOT IT.

TAP TAP

YOUR AMBULANCE IS HERE!

AND YOUR EXTRACTION TEAM.
TNT

FINE. GET HIM OUT, BUT NO DYNAMITE!

MIKE?

MIKE, IT'S GONNA BE FINE.

HANG IN THERE. WE'LL STOP BY WHEN YOU FEEL BETTER TO GET THE DETAILS.

WHAT ARE YOU THINKING?
SINCE MY SHORT TIME HERE, I DON'T KNOW WHAT TO THINK.

WERE YOU ABLE TO FIND OUT WHAT HAPPENED?
NO, HE WAS PRETTY OUT OF IT.

THE TRACKS LOOK LIKE HE DROVE THERE, **THEN** GOT FLATTENED.

CLUNK

WHY DOES IT SMELL LIKE HIPPIES?

BUZZZZ

BZZ
BZZ
DING DING
MIKE JUST GOT RELEASED FROM THE HOSPITAL. HE'S READY TO TALK TO US.

THANKS FOR THE UMBRELLA, ALFONZ.

OUI, MONSIEUR.

DOES HE HAVE HOSPICE?
NO, HIS WIFE IS THERE.

WIFE? EVER MEET HER?
NO. I UNDERSTAND THEY DON'T HAVE THE TYPICAL LOVE STORY.

NOTHING IN THIS TOWN IS TYPICAL.

NICE PLANT.

I FELT LIKE I NEEDED TO BRING SOMETHING.

KNOCK KNOCK

CREAAK

HELLO?

YES?

WE WORK WITH MIKE. THOUGHT WE'D CHECK IN ON HIM.

FOLLOW ME, HE'S IN THE LIVING ROOM.

HI GUYS!

HI MIKE.
HEY, BUDDY.

GOOD TO SEE YOU... ALIVE.

I THINK THEY MUST HAVE USED EVERY BANDAGE IN TOWN TO FIX ME UP.

UH...I THINK THEY MISSED A SPOT.
I THOUGHT I FELT A DRAFT.

I, UH, BROUGHT A PLANT FOR YOU.
JUST PUT IT WHERE IT LOOKS BEST.

IN THAT CASE, I THINK I'LL JUST PUT IT RIGHT HERE INSTEAD...
GULP GULP
THANKS.

I FOUND PAIN MEDS WORK BETTER WITH BEER.

BY THE WAY, THIS IS MAY. CAN SHE GET YOU SOMETHING? YOU'LL NEED TO USE SIGN LANGUAGE. SHE DOESN'T SPEAK MUCH ENGLISH. SHE'S A MAIL-ORDER BRIDE FROM CANADA.

SOME WATER WOULD BE GOOD.

DON'T CANADIANS SPEAK ENG...

NEVER MIND. WATER WOULD BE GREAT. THANKS, MAY.

YOU MIGHT HAVE NOTICED SHE'S A BIT ON THE SHORT SIDE. WHEN I PLACED MY ORDER I CHOSE THE CHEAPEST SHIPPING POSSIBLE.

MIND IF I CHANGE TOPICS? CAN YOU TELL US WHAT HAPPENED OUT THERE?

IT MIGHT NOT MAKE SENSE. NOT SURE IT DOES TO ME...

I WAS COMING HOME. IT WAS DARK AND I GLANCED AWAY FOR JUST A MOMENT.
WHEN I LOOKED UP, SOMETHING WAS STANDING IN THE MIDDLE OF THE ROAD...

I SWERVED, JUST MISSING IT. THAT'S HOW I ENDED UP IN THE DITCH.

SO YOU DIDN'T ROLL?

NOPE.

THEN WHAT CRUSHED YOUR TRUCK?
SAME THING I MISSED, I THINK.

CAN YOU DESCRIBE IT?

YOU'RE GONNA THINK I'M CRAZY, BUT IT LOOKED LIKE A MOOSE. BUUUUT, IT WAS WEARING OLD, RATTY CLOTHING.

ANYWAY, ONCE I HAD STOPPED, I LOOKED AROUND, THEN GOT BACK IN THE TRUCK TO CALL A TOW. THE NEXT THING I KNOW, WINDOWS ARE EXPLODING EVERYWHERE AND THE ROOF COMES CRASHING DOWN, PINNING ME LIKE A HUMAN PRETZEL.

HAVE YOU HEARD WE HAD SIX MORE DEATHS?

SIX?! I HADN'T HEARD THAT.

THIS TIME WE HAVE AN EYEWITNESS, BUT WE'RE A LITTLE SKEPTICAL OF HIS TESTIMONY. HIM BEING A HIPPY AND ALL, BUT HE DID DESCRIBE THE SAME THING AS YOU JUST DID.

SOOO, I WASN'T REALLY SEEING THINGS.

THIS CHANGES EVERYTHING. SAM, YOU KNOW WHO TO GO TALK TO.
YOU CAN'T BE SERIOUS.
'FRAID SO. TIME TO GET YOUR WENCH ON.

GET YOUR WENCH ON?

SO, JUST WHO IS THIS GUY WE'RE SUPPOSED TO TALK TO?

HE'S SOMEONE THAT'S SPENT A LONG TIME ROAMING THESE MOUNTAINS. IF THERE IS SOMETHING ODD GOING ON, HE'D BE THE ONE TO KNOW.

GANGRENE GULCH SALOON

HATE TO INTERRUPT YOUR BREAKFAST THERE, SALTYDOUGH, BUT MY PARTNER AND I NEED TO ASK YOU SOME QUESTIONS.

UH, SAM TELLS ME YOU'VE BEEN A MOUNTAIN MAN IN THESE PARTS FOR...

MOUNTAIN MAN?! THAT'S MOUNTAIN *PIRATE*, BOY!
I WOULDN'T CROSS A CREEK TO PEE ON A ***MOUNTAIN MAN*** IF HIS BEARD WERE ON FIRE! ***AARGH!***

SORRY. MOUNTAIN ***PIRATE***. MUST BE WHY THEY CALL YOU ***SALTY***DOUGH?

FEARED NOT!

THEY BE CALLING ME ***SALTY***DOUGH CUZ ME BREATH BE SO BAD, AFTER TALKING TO ME, YOU FEEL LIKE YOU'VE BEEN AS***SAULT***ED!

ACK!

THEY TELL ME MY BREATH SMELLS AS IF IT'S BLOWIN' OUT A ROTTED **BISON BUTT** PACKED WITH FESTERING **GARLIC** AND STRAINED THROUGH A RUSTY HUMIDIFIER!
TAHAAAARRR!

I BE GUESSIN' YOU AIN'T COME A QUESTIONING ABOUT ME ORAL HYGIENE.

NO, THAT'S BETWEEN YOU AND YOUR DENTIST. WE NEED TO KNOW ABOUT SOME STRANGE HAPPENINGS AROUND TOWN LATELY.

ARR, ENLIGHTEN YE I CAN. PREPARE YOURSELVES FOR A STORY SO DREADFUL & PUTRID, YOU'LL NEVER SLEEP AGAIN. DARK NIGHTS WHERE YOU CAN'T BE SEEIN' BUT INCHES IN FRONT OF YE OWN EYES. NIGHTS WHERE IT FEELS AS IF YOUR VERY SOUL COULD BE RIPPED OUT ANY MOMENT. THAT'S WHEN THE CREATURE BORN STRAIGHT FROM HELL PLIES HIS DASTARDLY TRADE.

THE VILE HELLSPAWN SEEKS ITS VICTIMS WITH NO THOUGHT OF MERCY. THE CRUEL ENTITY DESIRES ONLY ONE THING...FEAR!! IT FEEDS UPON IT LIKE ROSIE O'DONNELL AT A GOLDEN CORRAL BUFFET.

IT SETS ITS DARK SOULLESS EYES ON ITS PREY AND MOVES IN LIKE A GREASED CAT. STEALTHY, MEASURED, UNSTOPPABLE BY MORTAL MEANS...

IT GRIMLY SETS ABOUT TO INFLICT ITS EVIL ON HAPLESS SOULS. WORDS CAN HARDLY DESCRIBE THE WRETCHED DEEDS THAT BEFALL IT'S CLUELESS VICTIMS.

IT ALL BE TRUE! HAPPENED TO OL' SALTYDOUGH DALE HISSELF. FIVE TIMES THIS WEEK ALONE!

ACTUALLY, WE WERE TALKING ABOUT THE BIZARRE MOOSE MAULINGS.

MOOSE MAULINGS?

YEAH, ***NINE*** DEATHS IN JUST THE PAST FEW DAYS. WE WERE HOPING YOU MIGHT KNOW SOMETHING?

OH, THAT. MIGHT HAVE SOMETHING TO DO WITH A RIDICULOUS LEGEND 'BOUT SOME SUPERNATURAL MOOSE MAN THAT RISES UP AND KILLS PEOPLE OVER SOME ANCIENT WRONG OR ANOTHER. BEDTIME FODDER, IF'N YOU ASK ME.

KNOW WHERE WE CAN FIND OUT MORE ABOUT THIS RIDICULOUS LEGEND?
DUNNO. KILLER MOOSE RISES, GOES ON KILLING SPREE UNTIL SOMEONE STOPS IT. BLAH BLAH. TRY GOOGLING IT.

UMM.. YEAH.. WELL THANKS FOR THE INFO, SALTY..

SO... WHAT DO WE DO NOW?

WONDER HOW MANY HITS WE'D GET ON "HOMIDCIDAL MOOSE MAN?"

AH! WE COULD GO CHECK THE LIBRARY. I'M THE VOLUNTEER LIBRARIAN.
SURE.

LIBRARY

IT'S CLOSED.
USUALLY IS. THERE'S NOT A LOT OF READERS IN THIS TOWN.

LEAD THE WAY.
WHY ARE YOU WHISPERING.

IT'S A LIBRARY.

ACCORDING TO THE LEGEND, A HUNTING PARTY WENT OUT TO GET SOME MEAT BEFORE THE WINTER HIT. THEY CAME UPON AN EXTREMELY LARGE BULL MOOSE AND SHOT IT WITH AN ARROW. WOUNDED, IT RAN OFF WITH THE HUNTERS FOLLOWING. THE MOOSE HAPPENED UPON A SHAMAN GATHERING HERBS AND GORED HIM. THE HUNTERS SAW THE MOOSE RUN OFF WITH THE SHAMAN STUCK IN ITS ANTLERS. IT WAS BELIEVED A SOUL PACT WAS MADE FOR THEM. BOTH TO SURVIVE AND BECOME ONE. AFTER THAT, THE MOOSE MAN BEGAN TO TERRORIZE VILLAGES. MANY BRAVE WARRIORS DIED TRYING TO STOP IT. A SHAMAN FOUND A TEMPORARY WAY TO SEND THE MOOSE MAN TO THE UNDERWORLD. IF IT WAS RELEASED IT WOULD KILL AGAIN...

THAT'S IT... IT JUST ENDS...

NO HINTS ON HOW TO STOP IT?
NO! JUST ENDS. I MEAN, ***WHO*** WRITES A STORY ABOUT A KILLER MOOSE AND ***NOT*** PUT IN HOW TO STOP IT?

I MEAN YOU HAVE DRACULA, WOODEN STAKE. WOLFMAN, SILVER BULLET.

FRANKENSTEIN'S MONSTER, FIRE. THE MUMMY, WELL.. NOT SURE ON THAT ONE.

GILBERT GNOMISH

I KNOW WHO WROTE THIS BOOK **AND** HE JUST HAPPENS TO LIVE NEARBY.

MMMM...

SURE I CAN'T INTEREST YOU IN A CUP OF COFFEE?

NO, THANKS.

WE FOUND YOUR BOOK ON ALASKAN NATIVE LEGENDS.

WE WERE HOPING FOR MORE ON THE MOOSE MAN.

AH, MY LEGENDS BOOK. NOT A GREAT SELLER.

YOU MENTIONED IT COULDN'T DIE BY SPEAR OR ARROWS.
CORRECT. ANYONE THAT GOT CLOSE ENOUGH WAS VICIOUSLY TORN APART.

WHY SO INTERESTED IN THAT LEGEND?

WE HAVE GOOD REASON TO BELIEVE IT EXISTS AND IS KILLING PEOPLE. DOES THE LEGEND SAY ANYTHING ABOUT STOPPING IT?

SO, THERE **IS** SOME TRUTH TO THE LEGEND. IF IT HAS BEEN RELEASED, THEN IT CAN'T BE STOPPED LIKE BEFORE. IT HAS TO BE LEGITIMATELY KILLED.

ANNNNDD... HOW DO WE KILL IT.

AS LUCK WOULD HAVE IT, I'VE BEEN DOING EXTENSIVE RESEARCH ON THAT IN GREATER DETAIL. HERE'S A COPY OF MY *"LEGEND OF THE MOOSE MAN"* RIGHT HERE.

THIRTY BUCKS.

WHAT?!

THIRTY BUCKS. THIS IS AN ADVANCE COPY. DO YOU KNOW HOW MUCH RESEARCH I DID?

PEOPLE'S LIVES ARE AT STAKE!
MY DINNER IS AT STAKE. GOTTA MAKE A LIVING.

FINE...TAKE DEBIT?

DO I LOOK LIKE A STARBUCKS? CASH ONLY.

SLAM

WHO SHOULD I SIGN THIS TO?

A POP-UP BOOK?!

MARKETING. I TOOK A BATH WITH THE FIRST BOOK, SO I DECIDED ON A CHILREN'S POP- UP.

HAVE YOU READ THIS TO CHILDREN?
WATCH OUT!

NO. I'M READING IT TO A KINDERGARTEN CLASS NEXT WEEK.

GOOD LUCK WITH THAT.

WAIT! TO KILL THIS THING, YOU HAVE TO DRIVE AN ANTLER THROUGH ITS... ITS SPLEEN?

KINDA HARD TARGET. THAT'S WHY THE UNDERWORLD VERSION WAS ATTEMPTED.

SO WHY THE SPLEEN. DO MOOSE EVEN HAVE SPLEENS?

TURN THE PAGE.

How to kill a
oose monster....
Step 1: Hold **antlers** in attack position.
Step 2: Stab **spleen**.
Step 3: Moose is **dead**

THOROUGH BOOK.

THAT'S WHY I GET PAID THE BIG BUCKS.

ACTUALLY, I DON'T GET PAID THE BIG BUCKS. THAT'S WHY...

MERCHANDISE!! WOULD YOU LIKE A BOBBLE-HEAD MOOSE MAN? KEYCHAINS? PERHAPS A CANDY-POOPING MOOSE MAN?!

Park Ranger HQ
LATER THAT EVENING AT THE RANGER STATION...

GOOD EVENING, DEAR..

JUST HAVING A HARD TIME SLEEPING, SO I THOUGHT I'D DO SOME WORK.

DON'T MIND ME. YOU'LL NEVER KNOW I'M HERE.

NICE DECOR.
HANG IN THERE!
MORE OF A SURVIVAL THING THAN DECOR.

HANG IN THERE!
THWAK!

ZZZZZZZZZZZZZ...

NOW WE'RE OK.

WE NEED TO COME UP WITH A GAME PLAN.

MAYBE CALL FOR OUTSIDE HELP?

MAYBE I'LL TRY THE ALASKA STATE TROOPERS.

HELLO? THIS IS RANGER ZACK DEL POLLO FROM GANGRENE GULCH...YEAH, ALASKA.
LOOK WE'VE HAD SEVERAL KILLINGS AND NEED YOUR...

YES, **ALASKA**. I PROMISE YOU GANGRENE GULCH **IS** ON THE MAP. WE HAVE AN EMERGENCY, WE'VE.... NO, IT'S A SMALL PLACE. YES, WE ***ARE*** ON THE MAP. THE BIG ONES. LISTEN, WE'VE HAD MULTIPLE MURDERS.
BY **WHO**?

WELL...A MOOSE MAN. YEAH, HALF MAN & HALF MOOSE. ARE YOU ***LAUGHING***?! HOW DO I KNOW IT'S NOT A MOOSE ***WOMAN***? IT'S GOT ***HUGE*** ANTLERS!

HELLO? ***HELLO?***
CLICK

THEY HUNG UP..
CAN YOU ***BLAME*** THEM?

SO WE'RE SUPPOSED TO HARPOON THIS THING WITH ANTLERS IN THE SPLEEN. WHY THE SPLEEN?

MAYBE THAT'S WHERE ALL THE EVIL IS STORED?

IT'S ALL I GOT.

EVEN IF WE DO STAB THIS THING, HOW DO WE KNOW IT WON'T JUST PISS IT OFF MORE?

GOOD POINT. AND GETTING AN ANTLER TO STAB IT. EVER TRIED THAT? THIS ISN'T POKING A HOLE IN A SANDWICH, IT'S A LARGE, ANGRY KILLING MACHINE.

I'VE THOUGHT ABOUT THAT TOO. 100 YEARS AGO THEY CHOSE OPTION #2, AND **THEY** WERE TRAINED HUNTERS.

WE CAN'T DO THIS ALONE.
WE NEED TO GO TALK TO MIKE AGAIN. MAYBE HE'LL KNOW SOMEONE ELSE THAT CAN HELP.

IT'S GETTING LATE, SO WE SHOULD HEAD OVER NOW.

ZZZZZ

SOOTY
YOU WILL PREVENT FOREST FIRES!
OR I'LL GUT YOU
KE A BABY DEER!
JANUARY

YOU REALLY GONNA DRAG THOSE ANTLERS EVERYWHERE WE GO?
BETTER SAFE THAN SORRY.

AT LEAST YOU THOUGHT THAT FAR AHEAD.

MIKE'S GOTTA KNOW SOMEONE THAT CAN HELP. WE SHOULD CALL AHEAD.

I LEFT MY PHONE IN MY TRUCK...
MY PHONE IS DEAD..

GOOD THING THIS ISN'T A MOVIE, CAUSE THIS IS WHEN BAD THINGS HAPPEN.

*POP!

YOU WERE SAYING?

FLOP FLOP FLOP

I'LL GO CHECK THE DAMAGE...

OH, YEAH, IT'S A FLAT. POP THE TRUNK.

HEY! THIS IS WHERE MIKE WAS ATTACKED... SAME PULL OFF.

GREAT! LET'S CHANGE THIS TIRE QUICK AND GET OUT OF HERE.

GOT THE JACK. SPARE SHOULD BE UNDER HERE..

FOUND YOUR SPARE!

THIS IS **YOUR** CAR! WHAT ARE **YOU** DOING WITH A BIKE TIRE?!
WHAT ARE YOU DOING WITH A BIKE TIRE?!

I BOUGHT THIS CAR FROM JED A FEW MONTHS AGO. NEVER THOUGHT TO LOOK...

WELL... NOW WHAT DO WE DO?

WHAT ABOUT THE MOOSE MAN?

I'M SURE HE'S A LONG, LONG WAY FROM HERE.

AAAROOOOROOOAAARRR!

OOORRRRR... HE COULD BE NOT SO FAR AWAY...

THINK WE SHOULD STAY WITH THE CAR?
IT'D BE SHELTER FOR THE NIGHT.

REMEMBER MIKE'S TRUCK?
WHAT ARE THE CHANCES IT'D COME BACK THIS WAY?

MWROOOOARR!!

THAT'S WAS CLOSER.
I HAVE A FRIEND THAT'S BUILDING A CABIN BACK UP THE ROAD NEAR HERE.

SOUNDS GOOD TO ME.

HERE, HOLD THIS.

CRACK
CRUNCH!

HE'S COMING FROM OVER THERE...

ZACK, WE NEED TO GO NOW!

MWROOAAAAR!!

HOLY CATS! THAT'S WAS CLOSE!!

CLANG
CRUNCH
SMASH!

SOUNDS LIKE HE FOUND YOUR CAR, AND HE'S NO OLDSMOBILE FAN.

COME ON, SAM, OR YOU'LL BE NEXT!

AFTER WHAT FELT LIKE AN ETERNITY LATER...
THERE'S THE CABIN, JUST UP AHEAD.

REALLY?

DOES EVERYONE USE THE **SAME** CONTRACTOR FOR CABINS?!
IT IS SMALLER THAN I THOUGHT..

IT'S BETTER THAN NOTHING.

STOMP!

*SNIFF
SNIFF*

MMMGRRRR...

MMMRRRROOOAR!

WE NEED TO GET IN HERE!
YEAH, IT'S GOTTA BE TRACKING US.

SLAM!
THIS DOOR LOOKS STURDY ENOUGH...

OH...

WALL'S MISSING...

NOT GOOD.
EVIDENTLY, MY FRIEND STILL HAS SOME WORK TO DO.

RUN!

WHAM!

HE'S COMING!!

SLAM

OK.. NOW WHAT'S THE PLAN?

NOT TO DIE!

NO.
DO YOU HEAR HIM?
MWAROOOAAR
AHH!
FRACK!
AAAAAHHHHHH!

CRASH!

OOF!

UNH!

GO, GO, GO!

WHERE DO WE GO?

I DON'T KNOW! JUST RUN!

OOF!

GROWL...

UM... COULD YOU TELL ME WHERE YOUR SPLEEN IS...?

WHAMM!

I REALLY DIDN'T EXPECT THAT TO WORK...

RUN BEFORE HE GETS UP!

WE HAVE NOWHERE TO GO AND I'M DONE RUNNING!
WHAT ARE YOU DOING?!
HE'S GONNA SQUASH YOU LIKE A BUG!
A LITTLE CONFIDENCE PLEASE?
OH I'M CONFIDENT THAT..
OH CRAP! HERE IT COMES!

MMEAARRYAAA!!!

WHAM!!!
Grease Trap Cafe
If it ain't fried, it ain't food.
CRASH!!!
Grease Trap Cafe
If it ain't fried, it ain't food.

I WASN'T TEXTING AND DRIVING, I SWEAR!

HUH... SO THAT'S WHERE THE SPLEEN IS...

ALFONZ, ARE YOU...UH...OK?

I...I...DON'T KNOW...

SACRE BLEU! I CAN'T FEEL MY LEGS!

I THINK I'M STARTING TO FEEL BETTER...

MMMNNPHT, MMFFF, WHUMPMMHH!!

WELCOME TO GANGRENE GULCH. COME ON, BREAKFAST IS ON ME.

EDNA IS GONNA TAKE US BACK TO TOWN. JUST TRY TO KEEP HER AWAKE

YOU GUYS FINISH HERE. WE'RE HEADING INTO TOWN.

NO WORRIES, SAM.

YOU KNOW WHAT *I'M* THINKIN...?

YEP. **FIELD DRESS!!!**

OOSE MAN
URGERS
$10

A word about the artist:
Lucas Elliott

It seems you've found the "About the Artist" section! 5 points to Hufflepuff!

Ever since he was a wee lad, Lucas Elliott has been obsessed with the art of storytelling. Using imagery to tell a story has always had more of an effect on him than the actual wording has. With his work, Lucas tries to convey story and imagery through his use of action and line work. A lot can be said with very little.

Being in Alaska has given him a different viewpoint on the world and what comes and goes on a daily basis. He has always been intrigued by the mystery that is the tundra and just what lurks out there, which influenced him significantly when he was working on MOOSE.

Currently, Lucas is a freelance illustrator and character & concept artist based out of his igloo in Anchorage, Alaska. When he is not locked in the ice cavern he calls a studio, writing and illustrating his own stories, or working on projects for companies across North America, he is adventuring through the frozen wilderness with his wife and canine companion or watching cartoons. He's a HUGE fan of pizza, coffee, and discussing all that there is to comics, cartoons, and food. In fact, if you see him at one of the many conventions or shows he frequents and bring him these foods and conversation, he will become your best friend.

You can find more of his work on Facebook, Twitter, Tumblr or on his website at:

www.lucaselliottart.com

About the Co-Author: Darin Carpenter

Darin Carpenter currently lives in North Pole, Alaska with his beautiful wife Kristi. They have over a half dozen children, by last count, with the oldest being in the early 20's and the youngest being ages three, six and eight. Darin's hobbies are changing diapers and answering 2,000 questions a day that range from "Why can't I pick that off the ground and eat it?" to "How come I can't hit my brother with a rock?"

When not writing, he has also become a recognized master craftsman in the medium of super glue. There has been many an action figure that has benefited from his skill after a brief run-in with baby sister and her cute, pudgy little hands of doom.

Darin also enjoys warm summer evenings, pina coladas and locking himself in the bathroom in an attempt to get a few minutes of peace and quiet while also avoiding getting smacked with a plastic light saber for the 20th time.

About the other Co-Author: Chad Carpenter

Chad is best known as the cartoonist of the Internationally syndicated newspaper comic strip *TUNDRA,* which currently appears in over 650 newspapers around the world.

After many years of drawing comics, Chad decided it was time to inflict his imagination on the masses in an entirely different way. Thus, *MOOSE* the graphic novel and *MOOSE The Movie* were born.

Chad lives in Wasilla, Alaska with his fantastic wife, Karen and the two of his four children he hasn't managed to kick out of the house yet.

tundracomics.com & moosethemovie.com

You've read the book! Now watch the movie!

moosethemovie.com